Broken...
but not wounded

by

Charlene (La'Bet) Bardley Osatohanmwen

Charlene (La'Bet) Bardley Osatohanmwen

Copyright © Charlene (La'Bet) Bardley Osatohanmwen

All rights reserved. No part of this publication may be reproduced, distributed, or transmitted in any form or by any means, including photocopying, recording, or other electronic or mechanical methods, without the prior written permission of the publisher, except in the case of brief quotations embodied in critical reviews and certain other noncommercial uses permitted by copyright law.

Scripture taken from the New King James Version®. Copyright © 1982 by Thomas Nelson. Used by permission. All rights reserved.

The King James Version of the Holy Bible is in the Public Domain.

Scripture taken from The Message. Copyright © 1993, 1994, 1995, 1996, 2000, 2001, 2002. Used by permission of NavPress Publishing Group.

Book cover photo by: "Charles Mac" Dallas, Texas
Makeup by: ~Fernormenal Beauty, Anna. Texas
Hairstyle by Greg Hill, Mesquite. Texas

ISBN- 978-1-951300-44-9

Liberation's Publishing LLC
West Point - Mississippi

Broken...
but not wounded

Charlene (La'Bet) Bardley Osatohanmwen

Contents

- Foreword vii
- Dedication ix
- Acknowledgements xi
- Chapter 1 The Beginning 1
- Chapter II Finding a Friend 7
- Chapter III Open Door 11
- Chapter IV Moving Forward 19
- Chapter V Newest Edition 25
- Chapter VI New Beginning 37
- Conclusion 43
- Appendix 44

❧ Foreword

When I was first commissioned by Charlene, to write a forward for the book; "Broken but Not Wounded;" I was profoundly humbled and overjoyed to support, this awesome and anointed daughter in the faith. Once I completed digesting the life impacting pages of this carefully crafted manuscript, I discovered that "Broken but Not Wounded" is a must read for anyone in search of the righteous way to live in the midst of extremely difficult, pervasive, and sometimes crippling circumstances. It delineates how God can and does walk with His children through the fire (the thing designed to destroy) even when broken, and yet come out without a scratch (not wounded). Only our Lord God can do that. Hallelujah! B.B.N.W. is a how-to book on faith in the mist of mess, with a no-nonsense, straight-to-the-point approach. It's a powerful testimonial highlighting life-changing lessons that you can and will want to read in one setting. Hebrews 13:5 tells us that God will never leave us or forsake us. "Broken But Not Wounded" beautifully reminds us of this captivating truth.

Well done Minister Charlene (La'Bet) Bardley Osatohanmwen.

R T McKinney Jr. D. Min.
Senior Pastor, Redeeming Love Family Church

Charlene (La'Bet) Bardley Osatohanmwen

❧ Dedication

When I think of you, I see strength and endurance. You are strong and you never give up easy. You stood the tests of time no matter what you were facing. When the money was short, you still managed to have food on the table, clothes on our backs. God strengthened you every day just so you could be here today to encourage me. As I walked through the valley shadow of death (Psalm 24:4), you encouraged me.

Today mom, Lillie Washington Bardley, I dedicate this book to you. You have inspired me to walk in my truth and to help other women to become women of worth, integrity and humility. I honor you and desire to be the same type of mother to my daughter as you are to me. Your legacy lives on through me. You have instilled in me that living for Christ is the only way to bring your broken pieces back together.

Love you mother dear.

My dad, Jimmie Dale Bardley Sr., what words can I not say about you. From a little girl cannot have ask for more from a man. You helped mold and shaped me to be the person I am today! You had that strict discipline side that came from being in the Airforce. You brought that to our family, and it put the fear of God into us. We knew not to do wrong, or our back side would feel the wrath of God.

I lost my way on some occasions. I remember the lesson I learned when you disciplined me for going to the store during church. Though we had been told numerous times not to do this, there I was, caught red handed. I received the consequences behind it.

You told us about the life you had growing up, having only

one pair of boots. When your feet outgrew them, you had to cut the toes out just to get more wear out of them. You worked so hard so that we could have a better life. I could not even imagine your pain when you said how kids would make fun of you and say horrible things to you because your feet had a stench. I know this is one of the reasons today, I have so much heart for people who do not have.

    Love you dad!

❧ Acknowledgements

I want to first thank my Lord and Savior Jesus Christ who has and will always get the glory in all that I do! My husband Godwin Osatohanmwen, who pushed me and encourage me to complete this book. Even after it had lain dormant for several years before you came along into my life and helped me make peace with my past. My beautiful princess Patience Bardley Simmons whom I know God brought you into my life to serve. I know I could not have been so patient and calm through my storms without the peace you brought me. You would tell me every day to stop judging myself, love my imperfections every time I walked past my friend (the mirror lol). Mommy loves you!

Mother C. Meekins, I will never forget you for all that you and your family have done for Patience and me. You stood in the gap when there was lack. I thank God every day for you and your husband for getting on the road at three in the morning when Patience and I were stranded. The both of us were stranded between Fayetteville, NC, and Raleigh. I pray God will return to you one-hundred-fold.

Ms. Paulette you were an angel for taking care of Patience when I had to work those long twelve-hour shifts. I Thank You! Evangelist Queen Kemp, as a true woman from the Lord, you gave me words of knowledge on how to live as a godly woman with integrity, grace, and boldness. I will forever use your quote, "I get my instructions from Holy Ghost Headquarters!" Dr. RT and Louisa McKinney (Redeeming Love Family Church Fayetteville, Nc.) thank you for taking me under your wings and praying for me when I could not see the end. All I could do was keep coming to church to hear the word of God and let it strengthen me so that I could continue moving forward, Thank You!

The Jetta Family, thank you for your prayers and opening your home to me when I just needed rest. Shirley Turner & Family, Deborah Russel & Family, Ms. Monica Strong, Prestonwood Christian Academy, Joanne Hayes, Ms. Gayla, Ron & Tunisia Evans, Ms. Alma, Mr. Steve Butler, Ms. LaRachel, Mrs. Carolyn Jackson, Ms. Kay Ingram, Sherita Bardley, Mr. Craig & Tiffany Henson, Annette Washington, Apostle Sean & Prophetess Beverly Anike (Christ Purpose International Richardson, Texas), Northside MB Church (Columbus, Mississippi), Ms. Beverly Goodly & Dr. Edward Conway (One Community Church Plano, Texas), and Daphne Patmon Terry.

My parents have done a great job in raising us despite having to live in the Housing Projects at 1604 Clover Street in Columbus, Mississippi.

I can truly say those were some of the best memories. For all the families we connected with while residing in the projects, I would like to thank you for your part in help raising me to become the person I am today!
Broken But Not Wounded……

❦ Chapter 1 The Beginning

Charlene LA 'Bet Bardley born July fifth on a bright Sunday morning at two fifteen. I can remember the stories my mother would share with me of how I was born on that BIG day! She told me that my father and the rest of the family had gone to a picnic early the day before, July 4th. You know an event like the fourth of July is nothing but family, food, and fun! Yes, did I say "hot dogs, hamburgers, ribs, greens, beans, potatoes, tomatoes. You name it!" Ok bring it back that was "Shirly Caesar," lol. Well on that day of the fourth mom said she had such an awesome time, but once she got home that night, the food did not settle with her.

Later that night it paid off big time. Mom started having an upset stomach and could not rest. She thought she was feeling the backlash from all that food she had eaten. She got up and went to the bathroom. Well guess what! That food pain turned out to be little ole me trying to come out! I guess I wanted to see where the rest of the green beans, potatoes, tomatoes were and wanted more. My mother said she ran in the room and started screaming, "JIMMIE!!!!!!!!! Jimmie! Jimmie! Wake up! This baby is coming!" She said that my dad started panicking while trying to put his clothes on. He looked out of the window and a random woman (an angel) just happened to be walking down the street that morning. I was coming and they needed to hurry, and I mean hurry. I want to come out! My dad beckoned for the lady to come, and she did. In fact, they found out that the woman was a midwife. Wow! Thank you, Jesus!

"I believe nothing happens apart from divine determination and decree. We will never be able to escape from the doctrine of divine predestination. "The doctrine that God has foreordained certain people unto eternal life." (Charles H. Spurgeon) God ordered that lady to be where she was that night. As I look back over my life, I realized that even then God had already marked me for greatness. He had me covered from birth for all I was going to go through in my life. My parents needed help and what they got was a miracle from God. My midwife came in and helped bring me into this world full of sin and shame. My new home that God decided to birth me into was 1701 12th Avenue North Columbus, Mississippi 39701.

I always wondered how a child was born into a home without all the necessary equipment. For instance, when I see how children are brought into the world now compared to when I was born. Thinking back to when I was born, the midwife only needed a kitchen knife to cut the cord and her hand to smack me on my rear. All I had to do was let them hear me scream bloody murder to the top of my lungs. What about the mucus in my nose and whatever else they use today to "make sure babies are healthy?" Well, I guess through the passing of time they have decided that a smack on the butt is now considered child abuse lol. WE NEED MORE OF THOSE SMACKING THE BUTTS! Train up a child in the way they should go and when he is old, he will not depart from it, *Proverbs 22-6 KJV*.

I can remember growing up in Columbus, Mississippi. We moved to different projects homes as our family grew.

Between 1963 and 1972 we grew from one child to seven children, four boys and three girls. Jimmy Dale Jr. was named after our father, he was the first born, eldest son of my parents. He was very quiet and was not one to keep up noise. He was also the one to stand on neutral ground when it came to sibling rivalry.

James Fitzgerald was named after my dad's brother. He was the second eldest and had his own identity of life. James was direct and stood his ground. If you came to him wrong or felt like stepping to him, he was NOT the one to back down. He was a gentle giant in his own rights. He also had this joy about himself that even though was going through things no one would know. He allowed his inner strength to get him through it. James was not a burden to NO one. He made it happen.

Freddie is the third child and third son who was a mystery puzzle. I see Freddie as a person who wanted more in life. I think within his own self, failure was not an option. He wanted to succeed no matter what. Freddie was a person that just wanted to fit in. With that came a price of people trying to bully him as we were growing up, but BIG brother James would be there to rescue him.

Loretta is the fourth child and first daughter. Loretta Lynn, the name she gave herself, was a person who my mother saw as a little princess. Mom wanted to give her all the pretty things life had to offer her. Pageants, piano lessons, record players, easy bake ovens and the list went on of things she had. Loretta was the sister I looked up to and admired because of the go getter she was. Loretta and Fred wanted to make a legacy for themselves. She had high standers and goals that she wanted to achieve. She knew that she did not want to be known as a person from the projects, so she decides at a young age by any means necessary she was going to make it out of the projects and SUCCEEDED. She did just that according to Colossians 3:23, "whatever you do, work heartily, as for the Lord and not for men." NKJV I was so proud of her that I looked up to her as my role model. I saw her as this beautiful young lady. I admired her inner beauty.

Sharon Sha'Kaye was the fifth child and second daughter. Sharon was this little timid little girl. A fly or net would make her run for dear life. It trained her, literally that is who she was a TRACK star. Yes, Sharon was good as a runner, but lacked the confidence that would propel her into life. Sharon would not leave her comfort zone, and I believe that has kept her back from achieving more in life. Sharon was one of the siblings that stayed under mother dear and needed that reassurance of belonging. I knew Sharon could do so much. Even though life may have thrown her curve balls she still went on and obtain her master's degree.

Now this little boy the last of the Bardley bunch. Heath, the seventh child and fourth son was quite a challenge for all of us. He was spoiled, and whatever he wanted he knew how to get it! Heath was my shadow. He and I were the last ones at home. The other siblings were gone to school, and we created a bond that still exist today. If you need help and it doesn't matter how you have wronged him, he still will find it in his heart to step up and help you. I have seen people talked about him and back stabbed him, but regardless of the circumstances he still would set his pride down to help. Proverbs 6 (KJV).

As his big sister when he would need my help no matter where I was in life or doing, I would always be there to rescue him out of his mischiefs, lol. Once he got hit on the head with a bed rail and it left a big gash down his head. I would work so that he would not fall in that peer pressure of becoming a thug or hanging in streets of our small town. I even gave him an allowance so that he would not get into trouble. I am proud of the man God has birth him to become.

Don't you see that children are Gods best gifts? The fruit of the womb his generous legacy. Like a warrior's fistful of arrows are the children of vigorous youth. Oh, how blessed are you parents, with your quiver full of children! Your enemy do not stand a chance against you; you will sweep them right off your doorsteps Psalms 127:3-5 (MSG).

Charlene (La'Bet) Bardley Osatohanmwen

❧ Chapter II Finding a Friend

In the word of God, Jesus is a friend who sticks closer than a brother (Proverbs 18:24) NIV. I can remember my friend Kim, who she and I was inseparable growing up in the projects. We would play outside sunup till sundown after school and on the weekends. When we came home from school, we would be able to come outside just for a little minutes before supper time yes, we folks from the South called evening meals supper time lol. I enjoyed her friendship at an early age because she had a genuine friendship and we played well together. We never were allowed to go into each other's house growing up and I think looking back at that, this allowed us to be more outside getting fresh sunlight and fresh air that seems to make you have that outdoor odor once you enter back into your house. This did not bother us that we could not go into each other homes because if Kim and I were able to play outside it was just fine.

Kim had two older brothers, so it was three of them out of our Big #7. Kim was the only girl and I guess I was like a sister she never had. I believe at that time Kim, and I was in the second or third grade and we attended Union Academy school. Even though she and I was not in the same classrooms going to school to see other friends was still fun and exciting but knew when that bell ranged, we would be back at it playing outside in our back yards. A man who has friends must be friendly, but there is a friend who sticks closer than a brother Proverbs 18:24 (NKJV).

I could remember one day as Kim and I was playing outside, she told me the most dreadful news a little 8- or 9-year girl could wrap her tiny brains around. Kim and her family were relocating to California. What!!! California! Who is this California and why is she taking you away from me? I did not or could not now think of why they would be moving since it appears that they were happy living there. You see growing up in my area we did not see families move far away only from one of the open project homes to another project home because their family outgrew their homes. California was about 31 hours and over 2.000 miles away from me so how was Kim and I going to play after school?

No, Kim would not be playing after school anymore nor will she be attending my school. This was so for real that all I could do was cry because I had bonded with this person and now what will I do and who would become my best friend? I started thinking of a song by the late Andrae' Crouch, "Jesus Is the Answer for the World Today."

Song like this had meanings and still resonates with my spirit then and now. Kim and I from that point on made sure every moment we would play after school and continue to bond as much as possible until we could not play anymore.

It seems like forever for her to moved that it reminded me of when your parents told you that you were due a spanking and you knew it was going to happen, but you just did not know when. We were already in school and then all the holidays came and gone, and we were on the other side of the school year that it was almost May, and my little heart was like well its passed April and I thought they would have used that month to say surprise this has been an April fool's joke but just as the last day of school and the weekend roll around, it was this Big truck that had the words U H A U L written in Big Bold letters pulled up in front of Kim's house! Oh No!!! what is going on? I thought this was not going to happen because several months had passed. What I found out was Kim's family was waiting for school to end so that they could move doing the summer months.

The process was now so real and the packing of the UHAUL has now begun. I saw chairs, and clothes being put into the UHAUL. I felt my heart being smashed but that did not stop Kim and I from continuing to playing outside. Every day was another day but soon it was winding of them now cleaning the house out with all the items in the truck. It has finally come to an end they were finish and now it was time for them to take that journey to California. I do not know what time of the day Kim left but that day I did not get a chance to see Kim off and now she was gone forever.

"People come into your life for a reason, season, are a lifetime." For everything there is a season, and a time for every matter under heaven Ecclesiastes 3:1 (ESV). It never was explained to me why people move far away from people who cared about them. It was never explained to me that it was common for people to move away and that one day you will see them again. I believe if someone had of sat me down and explain those things it would not have been such a trauma for me of feeling a since of an abandonment. So many people in life have had someone to abandoning them and this has caused so much pain and sorry to the point of nervous break downs, relationship concerns, or even suicide. You may be broken but you are not wounded!

❦ Chapter III Open Door

Weeks had gone by since they moved, and every day seemed long and boring to the point I was inside more than outside. Yes, true I had my family, but they had their own friends. I wanted nothing to do with their friends because I wanted to have my own friends.

We had family time where we would go visit our relatives but the moment, we got back home all I saw behind my home was an empty house waiting for another family. The questions were, will they have someone I could play with, or would I have just as much fun as the previously friend, or will they just have boys? Those were the questioned I was left with.

As time went on, I believe a family did move in, but there were no girls to play with. So, what was I to do? I finally sucked it up and just gradually started hang outside with my dolls and jacks to occupy my time.

Then one day! A little girl came over from out of nowhere and ask if she could play with me. I was like, "where did she come from and where have she been hiding?" I was so longing to play that I did not care where she came from. She introduced herself as Demarx (I will refer to her as Dee going forward.) Dee told me she attended Union Academy, but I had never seen her at school and had no idea we were in the same grade! I was so shocked to also find out that she lived right across the streets from the projects. It was just, as the people in the South would say, a skip and a hop! Wow, all this time I was feeling as though I would never have a friend to play with, and she was right here all the time.

Dee had two brothers and two sisters, and she was the eldest of them all. I was so happy to finally have someone to play with. It took my mind off Kim leaving. Dee and I would play just like Kim, and I would. We'd play outside and running around. It was so great that if Dee had been an alien, it would not have matter because I had a friend. I played so much over the summer months that it never dawned on me to ask Dee what she had been doing, or why I had not seen her before at school, or even out playing with other kids.

It seems so strange that Dee was never seen outside during play time. One day out of nowhere, Dee did come out to play. She came and asked me if I knew how to kiss. At first, I was so blown away. I was in the fourth grade, and that was something I had never been asked. I mean I saw my parents kiss around the house or have affection for each. This was different, for a child to ask me such things blew me away! I guess after realizing I had no idea what she was going with this question, she asked me if I would like her to show me. I hesitated. But, then in a small voice I said, "Yes sure!"

I really had no idea exactly what I was getting ready to get involved in. I tried just ignoring the fact that I responded yes hoping this would blow over. But then she says, "Hey let us go to my house." You must realize all of the time Kim and I were friend I had never gone to her house. Let alone anyone else, this was forbidden by my parents. Before the thought had finished processing, Dee had grabbed me by my hands. We walked over across the street to this big house that was all by its lonesome self. I had never seen that house before in my life. Maybe it was because I had no reason to look over there before. I had always played with Kim. I never paid any attention to it.

We walked to her house and entered in. Her siblings were watching TV sitting on sofas.

I wanted a friend, so I followed Dee around her home. I remember it was very cold and dark in the house. I do not know where her parents were, but apparently Dee knew what time they would be home. Dee led me to a bathroom and locked the door behind us. I did not know what was about to take place but waited to see what she was going to do. She than started kissing me on the lips. I was so not sure what I was supposed to be doing, so I started to mimic what she did to me. That went on for about one to two minutes and then I ran home.

I did not know exactly what had just happened, but I was pretty sure my mother would not have liked it. I would have been in a lot of fish grease trouble. First, I went inside someone's house without my parents' permission and with NO PARENTS AT HOME! Talking about the seat of my pants would still have been burning today. All for the sake of being curious and having a friend. I was brought up in a Baptist church and the preacher got up there every Sunday and strongly reminded us of Adam and Eve.

I could hear the Pastor preaching, "God put Adam into a deep sleep and from his rib he took and created a woman whom he presented her to Adam, and he named her Eve. She was bone of his bone and flesh of his flesh." Genesis 2:21-23.

Going forward, it was a challenge to play with Dee every day because of what had transpired with us. I was only looking and needing a friend. I realized what we sometimes search for can be something that we do not need. I still tried to be her friend even through this little secret her and I shared. *There is nothing hidden that will not be disclosed and nothing concealed that will not be known or brought out unto the opening Luke 8:17 (NIV).*

Everything that Dee had done to me was now trying to manifest in me as a little girl. It caused me to want to kiss and recreate the same gratification of what happened in that bathroom. I now wanted to do the same thing to other girls. I noticed that our playtime went from playing outside to always going to her dark house and ending up in that old run-down bathroom. It advanced. We went from kissing to getting on top of each other with our clothes on. Today it would be considered sexually grinding. I came to understand I was trying to keep a friendship and forget about my loss of the friend who left me and moved to California.

I was glad when vacation bible school started at my local church, Northside Missionary Baptist. This allowed me to hang out and forget about this thing I was experiencing with Dee. I do not know how children could just sit in a dark house and not have friends they could hang out with. I knew I came up with loving parents and siblings that would have fell to their knees and cried for what was happening to me. I could not fathom in my head how to reach out to any of them for being judged.

Summer was almost over, and I was now headed to the sixth grade. I was going to meet new friends and leave this ugly thing behind me. A new school would give me an opportunity to play as a little girl was supposed to. I did not know if Dee would have any classes with me but who cares if I was at school. I had other people to play with.

So off I go to school on a summer evening as I did for the past years. We students would go to the hall of our grade and find our names on the door of the class we were in. We would meet our teacher for that school year. This was so much fun. It was exciting to meet because you got to meet your teacher and see all your classmates for the first time that year. I entered my class and guess what? Dee was in my classroom! I did not care too much because I knew that I loved school, and I was ready for it to start.

During the school year I had Mrs. Montgomery as my teacher. I loved class and loved learning. I was focused on school so much that hanging with Dee after school became less and less. Going back to that dark house was beginning to fade away. It helped that I had other children to be around. We played at school and that was about it. School was a safe place because it gave me the opportunity away from my predator. I came to realize that, yes even at that young age, she was a predator. She preyed on me. As I look back over it all and what had happened, I have realized that what Dee had done to me was apparently done to her.

So, if the son makes you free than you are unquestionably free John 8:36 (Amplified Bible). For all the young children that are going through what I had gone through at 8-9 years old please help these children to know that they can come to you and will not be judge or condemned of being preyed upon. Therefore, there is now no condemnation for those who are in Christ Jesus.

After that school year my family moved into another apartment, and it was time to head to seventh grade. Yay! Hunt High Middle School here I come! No more elementary but now a pre-middle schooler. There at this school we had children across town to come and that allowed me to meet new kids and move forward. Praise the Lord! New friends, new school, and lots of things to get involved in. I loved to sing, and since I had a fresh start, I sang in my local church choir. The spirit of newness had taken over my body! I loved being at school and it showed on my report cards. Yes! I had all A's and B' s. Wow! I was really doing it. My grades were so great that when school was out for the summer, I was able to go to El Paso, Texas to stay with my Uncle Jerry.

Uncle Jerry was a tough military man, but I was ok with that, because I was leaving Columbus. I was going to have lots of fun with my cousin Mary! Mary was originally from Germany. When my uncle met her mother, and we were around the same age. Uncle Jerry (RIP) was a strict military, discipline, type of man that walked and talked the military lingos. He was a make your beds and do what I say type of soldier. We dared not try him. I do not know why kids try to test the waters, but that was what Mary, and I did one day.

Her parents were having a gathering at their home. While the adults were having social time, Mary wanted us to sneak out of the house to go and visit some boys. What?! I do not know why I agreed, but again it seems like an adventure. Let's Go! We locked her bedroom door and out the window we went. We walked down the streets like giggling little girls about to find some treasure. We got there to her friend's house and stayed for a little bit. Soon we had to get back. We didn't know how long my uncle would be entertaining his friends. What we thought was about ten to fifteen minutes, turned into over an hour.

Mary and I got back to the house and tried to get back through the window. Little did I know Mary had been doing this often. Uncle Jerry apparently knew the game and opened the lock on the bedroom door and latched the window back! Did I say BIG TROUBLE!

We had no choice but to ring the doorbell. My butt was in Uncle Jerrys hands. *Whoever spares the rod hates his son, but he who loves him is diligent to discipline him Proverbs 13:24 (ESV)*. This is exactly what was about to take place with Mary and I, the rod was going to come down on us. I was already feeling my bottom turning red.

Mary and I went into the room and Uncle Jerry came in behind us. He carried this enormous belt from the military and began the spanking with Mary. I mean beat down. Uncle Jerry did not hold back at all. He went from left to right, up and down, and when I say left, right, up, and down it was just that. He did not care where that belt landed. I was already crying and screaming for my mother. Mary was running everywhere in the home in the shower and behind doors, but the belt continued. Well, guess what it? It was my turn, and I knew this was not going to go so well. I was screaming for my life and begging and pleading for him to stop. I did not get this type of beating at home, so all I could do was just take this whipping. I knew when it was all over, I was going to call my mother to get me home.

That is exactly what I did, get home. The next day I asked my auntie if she could call my mom. I told my mother what my uncle had done, and she told my uncle to put me on the next Greyhound bus back to Columbus, Mississippi. I was only thirteen or fourteen years old. I guess my mom felt confident that I could get home safely. I was on the next bus smoking. You better not play with Lille B. children lol. Once I got to Jackson, Mississippi I knew I was doing good. If anything happened to me, I was safe. I had family there.

I finally got home, and mom was waiting on me at the bus station. She did not give me any harsh talk, but welcome me with loving arms. What mistakes I had made in Texas were left in Texas. I came to a home that was full of love that my mom always seems to give to everyone.

I was broken but not wounded.

❧ Chapter IV Moving Forward

Even though my vacation was cut short, I still had time to come back and meet some friends. We just hung out before the new eighth-grade school year. I connected with a friend name Terrella "Bam" Madison, who lived not too far from me. My family moved to a new place close to her house. So, when I got back, she and I started hanging out and became close friends. She loved to sing and I as well. As the summer started winding down it was time to get our new schedule for the upcoming school year. Yes, we were now on our way to Joe Cook Middle School. That was one step from being in High School.

We were all moving forward. What had happened over the summer was a thing of the past. I was looking forward to meeting my teachers and connecting back with old friends from our old school. August could not get here fast enough. I was ready to start school, I had done so well in seventh grade. Well, school began, and I jumped right in.

After a couple of months, I realize that I needed to really study for my classes. I was having such a hard time and my grades were becoming worse and worse. I was starting to feel like a failure. I was joking around in class so bad I failed some needed classes. At the end of the school year, I had to go to summer school and make up those classes to advance to the ninth grade

I had to really work hard over the summer. That caused me to miss out on summer breaks and fun times. I do not know why no one sat me down and asked, "Charlene what is wrong, or why are your grades horrible?" I just had to find my why and figure it out all by myself. I did the work in summer school and that allowed me to advance to High School. It was sweet melodies to my ears. Stephen D. Lee High School (Go Generals) was my next adventure coming into my freshman year. We were called crab, fish, and anything else that fit us as Freshmen we heard it all. It did not bother me. I was in High School, and that was already an honor. Being in the ninth grade was the beginning of meeting new and exciting people. I was now in the big league of mature boys and girls. As school began, I reconnected with Dee since I had not seen her in forever months. She seems like she was doing good. We chatted here and there at school since we did not have the same classes.

We started walking to school together. Her family moved near me, and she had to pass my home in route to get to school. High School was so refreshing, and it looked like we all were on quest in our new chapter in life. School was about six weeks in, and this one-day Dee and I walked home as always. She said I must show you something. I did not know what this something was. She lifted her shirt, and I was so stun that I jumped back with so much of surprise that I almost got hit by a car.

I did not know what to say or do for that matter. I just put my hands over my mouth in disbelief. Dee was pregnant! We were only fifteen years old. I knew I was a virgin, and never knew Dee was having sexual relations in a manner to become pregnant. I was sworn to secrecy, but things like this have a way of coming out. I did not know how this was going to be kept a secret. What I did know was that one day that baby would have to come out.

After a couple of more months, I notice Dee started wearing larger shirts. We were walking home from school one day and she told me that her mother knew that she was pregnant. I was so relieved of this secret because I knew the risk for her and the unborn child. Anyway, the news was out. Months passed and it was time for her to have the baby. Once she had the baby, she was no longer able to attend school. I continued focusing on my education and just being a normal kid in school.

I than met a young man name Bobby, and he was an upper classman yes. I saw this fine "High Yellow" as they say in the South upper classman, and we hit it off well. I could not date because dating was not allowed. I had the fear of my parents in my soul. So, dating him was only allowed Monday thru Friday lol. This felt like a full-time job with those hours. When the weekend came around, I had no dealings with him. That sucked because there were parties I could not attend. All of the "bad" girls were there. So, eventually I would lose Bobby because first, I was not putting it out to him and secondly, I was not allowed to see him on the weekends. The bad girls got a hold of him.

Being from a strict family home had its pros and cons. I did not like the cons because I felt like I was missing out on being with friends and having a great time. Little did I know those pros helped me out a lot in becoming who I am today. *Train up a child in the way he should go, and when he is old, he will not depart from it Proverbs 22:6 (KJV)*. Bobby moved on with another girl, and I got back into my singing

Oh, how I love to sing, I knew when I was feeling a certain way about life, I would put me some music on and just soak in it as I sang to the melodies of any songs. As Kirk Franklin sings a song, "Melodies from heaven Rain down on me." I was a church girl, and I always knew when things in life seemed hard, I knew one place I could go to and that was church. That is where I found my sanctuary and sanity in the church!

Even when I was in the ninth grade, I chose the choir, and I loved it so much. I loved my choir teacher MS. Buckhalter and I felt we got along well as teacher and student. Ms. Buckhalter liked me so much that she chose me to choreography the dance routines for our upcoming choir performances for the school. Wow! Me? Yes, little ole me was chosen to do something!

The choir performances were such a hit that we all were so proud of ourselves and got great reviews from our peers. It seems like when I am on a high and things are going great the enemy comes in to block my blessings. *The thief cometh not, but for to steal, and to kill, and to destroy I am come that they might have life, and that they might have it more abundantly John 10:10 (KJV).* That is exactly what the thief came to shadow my love for music in the form of selling candy bars.

Well, we had to sell candy and I was giving a box to sell but I did not do it. I was lazy and thought the candy would sell itself. My mother had always told us not to bring products home to sell because it was so many of us that she did not have time to do it. So, the candy stayed on my dresser until Ms. Buckhalter asked for the money.

Oh my! What was I to do? I brought the candy back, and she told me that she needed the money. She could not accept the candy back too much time had passed. Why did I get rebellious with the one person who believed in me? She saw my talent and allowed it to be used. It was my pride. It also caused me to no longer be in choir the next year. I should have made better choices. Sometimes in life we want to be the person who is always be in the right. All it would have taken was humility and explaining why I could not sell the candy. I should have given it back in a better time frame. *Humble yourselves, therefore, under the mighty hand of God so that at the proper time he may exalt you 1Peter 5:6 (ESV).*

Ms. Buckhalter gave me the candy back and told me to take it home and bring the money back. When I got home Lille B. was not hearing such things. You know back in the days the parents could call the teachers on the telephone, and that's exactly what mother dear did. My mom expresses to Ms. Buckhalter that she was not selling the candy, nor was she going to buy the candy, and that she will be sending the candy back to school the next day!

What have I done? I have started an unnecessary battle, which should not have been open. I went to school the next day and humbly gave her the candy. She took the candy, and I thought all was well. I finished the school year out strongly. Well, the next year when it was time to get our schedule, guess who did not get in choir? Me! Yes, even though I finished that year out I was still held accountable for my behavior from the previously school year. *So then, each of us will give an account of himself to God, Romans 14:12(NIV).*

I had a passion and when you have a passion it burns inside that cannot be shaken. When it is destined for your gifts to shine than what's inside of you will come out no matter what the devil tries to do against you. *The thief comes only to steal and kill and destroy. I came that they may have and enjoy life and have it in abundance John 10:10 (AMP).* Even though the devil tries to take please know that he will not do any more than God allows him.

I know some of you might be feeling as though when will I get it back? I am here to tell you to keep looking to the hills from which cometh your help. Your help cometh from God up above.

I was so far to left after this situation happened in my life that my sophomore year was not going well. It showed in my grades. All I wanted to do was sing and now going to school was no longer satisfying. I was not living to my fullness at school, and I felt my passion going down the drain.

I was Broken but Not Wounded.

❦ Chapter V Newest Edition

My sophomore year start turning around with my friends Debra Porter, Colleen Martin, Terrella Madison, and Laquita Hill. We got together and formed a group called Newest Edition after the R&B singing group "New Edition" from the early '80's. Oh how we loved Ronnie, Bobby, Ricky, Mike, and Ralph Tresvant (lead singer). We wanted to have the fame like they did, and we were well on our way. The group started performing at our local schools and local talent shows. Everyone loved us. We even found a local manager who called himself "Snake" who had a dance group called (23rd street Snake Breakers).

Snake had us all around town and local areas as far as Memphis, Tennessee. The only thing was that we sang with the music. We did not know how to take the voices off the record for the judges to hear our voices and our real talents. People wanted to hear you not the people who created the songs. Our success was not doing so well.

We did not have any connections, and we were going down the drain very fast. We reverted to our local talent shows. I wanted the fame so bad that I knew in my heart that success had my name written all over it. I think I was pushing hard, but some of the girls started dating thinking this was not worth it. We still would find talent shows, but sometimes it would not be all of us.

When the rest of the group could not attend, I knew I could count on Terrella AKA "Bam." We went as a duo! We were doing great with the shows. We were going around town to perform, but people just did not gel to our talents. One day someone told us about this guy named Jackie. They said that we should go and allow him to listen to our group. My mother loaded us all up and went to meet this man name Jackie! Mr. Jackie B. would play the music so we would listen to the songs. Afterwards, we were to sing it acapella.

We tried and tried to make this happen, and sometimes we got frustrated. There were no connections in Columbus and there was nobody willing to help us local teenage girls. All I know is that I wanted and could see a vision of success for myself, but the how was I going to do this is what was lacking. *A man's heart plans his course, but the LORD determines his steps (Proverbs 16:9 ESV).*

I finally stop putting my life in a web going around and around in a circle to get my heart shattered. When you keep trying, I thought the saying was "If at First You Don't Succeed, Try, Try Again" is a fantasy short story by Zen Cho. It was first published on the official Barnes & Noble blog, in 2018. I tried and tried but no door would open for me. A cycle started again my grades started slipping. My friends were all moving in their gifts and talents. Here I was stuck in "cannot find my way." My grades were showing how I felt and again I had to go to summer school to help advance me to the next grade, Senior in high school.

My junior year went by so fast that while I was trying to be the next Whitney Houston, I was not paying attention to my classes let alone my grades. So, during the summer I hustled to make up my grades and worked hard. In the end, it paid off. I did not have to make up some courses as a senior, because I did it over the summer. One of the things I realize is that if you play when you first get to high school you will have to work extra hard your last year in school. That is what happen to me. I had to suffer the consequences. I had to ask Jesus to take the wheel. My last year the subjects were a little bit challenging to me like math and history. They were not subjects I wanted to jump up and down about or scream out. I can do it. It was just a matter or wanting to. *If I trust in the Lord and lean not to my own understanding in all my ways acknowledge him and would direct my path (Proverbs 3:5-6 KJV)*

During my Junior and Sophomore year I met a young man name Levatus at his church choir day. I dated him till I graduated in 1989. He graduated in 1988. Levatus went on to college and after one year he went on to join the US Army. This opened an old wound. There was something about when someone left me it opened past hurt of abandonment even though that was not the case. It felt like he had left me. While he was away, I was young and would still hang out with friends. I tried hard to not date other people, but I wanted someone in my life. All my friends were dating someone. I really do not know what he was doing there in Germany. I could hear my good friend Joann Allen who would say this repeatedly, lol.

It was my big time to get that PAPER (my diploma)! I was sooo excited that this day had finally came. I was about to cross over to achieve one of my goals in life despite the struggles. *Therefore, since we are surrounded by such a great cloud of witnesses, let us throw off everything that hinders and the sin that so easily entangles. And let us run with perseverance the race marked out for us (Hebrews 12:1 NIV).* When you look at this scripture it helps guide you to not give up. Whatever you are desiring on your life, once you have set your eyes on it, no matter what obstacles come your way, see it till the end.

So many of you have started this journey of life, but when it got hard you threw in the towel and gave up! I want to encourage you to pick up the book, your marriage, your child and say to it "I WILL SEE THIS TILL THE END!" A cake is not good until it has gone through the process and when it is finish you can enjoy the end results of your slaving in the kitchen.

I was not ready to settle down but held on to Levatus. I did not want to hurt him by leaving him. It is something about people leaving you, but when it comes to leaving them, we do not have the gift of goodbye. We stay in relationships that no longer serving a purpose, while expecting God's hand to produce a harvest when the soil is dry, and no life to see fruits coming forward. I took a breakout of school and did a little travel here and there.

I started dating Johnny who I had met in a club, and we hit it off! He was a little bit older than I was, but it was just to occupy my loneliness until Levatus came back. I would marry him. That did not go so well. I would eventually start driving to Alabama to see him or he would drive and see me in Columbus. I still had it in my head that I would marry Levatus, even though I was seeing someone else. *A double minded man is unstable in all his ways. (James 1:8 KJV).*

I was not stable. I was wanting to make everyone happy and could not find the gut to stop and release one man and see another man. *The steps of a good man are ordered by the LORD, And He delights in his way (Psalm 37:23 NIV).*

How can a man be happy when his steps are not being order by the Lord? I continue dating Johnny and eventually Levatus was to come home for a month. Do in that time frame

I planned a wedding. "Hahahahah" what a wedding? Well, I did, and we got married. After he left to go back to Germany, I found myself hanging out with my friends and creeping back to see Johnny. I never told him I had gotten married. I was sinning and going straight to hell for my actions. I should have never done such a thing.

"How was I going to get out of this?" I expressed to my mother. "I have made a big mistake and wanted out!" My mother expresses to me that I had to stay in this relationship. I would hurt this person (mother was so compassionate) I stayed in this marriage. Eventually Johnny found out and ended the relationship.

I did not want to be married. It showed through my actions. I entered a new relationship with Patrick who had just moved to Columbus from Detroit! Well, I was determined to have a good time, because I felt I was robbed of my teenage life by marring at a young age. I wanted out, but my mom was not hearing of this! So, until Levatus came back, Patrick wine and dine me like the queen I was desperately desiring to be. He was kind, sweet, and romantic and did I mention a "Light Skinned brother."

I had a thing for men that were of a fair complexion and always loved their skin tones. Oh sorry, let me come back to reality. I Was Married and now Levatus was coming back to the states in a months' time. We would be moving to Monterey, California. Ok, how was this going to play out and how was I going to get out of this relationship? *For our struggle is not against flesh and blood, but against the rulers, against the authorities, against the powers of this dark world and against the spiritual (Ephesians 6:12)*

I had weaved a web and I needed my life to change and

needed Jesus to help me. God was still there, but I could not hear him because of the loud white noises in my ears of fun, clubs, and relationships. *For God so loved the world that he gave his one and only son that whosoever believeth in him shall not perish but have everlasting life (John 3:16 KJV).*

I knew I could lean on my faith because of the word of God that was in me from my mother and my church. I had to lean on this to ask to get out and I did just that. I told Patrick that I was leaving and would be moving to California with Levatus. I hurt Patrick, and what I was not expecting was him pulling out a ring as Johnny did in the past and asked me to marry him. I knew I had to make the right decision and decline that offer and walk away so that I could live in peace and in alignment of what God had created me to be.

Demons are real and I never delt with the issues of my past that laid dormant waiting on the right time to show up in my life. It was ABANDOMENT. I let everything go and packed up and moved to Monterey with Levatus. While in California, I went through mentally. Depression came upon me. I started thinking about that dark house, kissing Dee in her bathroom. I was sick to my stomach, and I reverted to that afraid little girl and feared someone finding out that this had happened to me.

I enrolled in college there and that was the best thing for me. I was trying to put those pieces back together again. Levatus and I were not getting along. I was always angry and miss my family. Levatus got orders to go to war, and he was going to be gone for over a year! Here I go again away from family. Now I must be across the world by myself alone.

I dug into my books and eventually met Carolyn Jackson (from Georgia); her husband was away as well. She and I started hanging out and enjoying the Monterey sunshine. We became good friends. She would give me advice on the military lifestyles, and as of today she and I still maintain a close friendship. After Levatus came back, we got orders to move to Killeen, Texas. Yes Lord! I was closer if I needed to see my parents and I was so happy. We settled in and a couple of years passed Levatus, and I started growing apart.

I found my joy with Christ as we went through marriage issues as young couples do. I started gaining weight from depression. The depression came from me doing things in my life and not being truthful to Levatus. It came because of the masked I was wearing. *(Hebrews 4:13, NLT): "Nothing in all creation is hidden from God. Everything is naked and exposed before his eyes, and he is the one to whom we are accountable."* I was hitting around 200 pounds and ate my hurt and pains away.

Some may be going through darkness in your life, and many have some sins and skeletons in your closets even today. I am here to encourage you and let you know that you are not alone. *Whom the son sets free is free indeed (John 8:36 NLT).* Levatus did his six years in the military and eventually met someone else and moved on by divorcing me in 1998. We had purchased a home in Killeen, and I was awarded the house. The very thing I had wanted in the past came into my future.

You see even though I wanted it back then, it showed up in my future later in life. Be careful of what you put in the atmosphere. *Death and life are in the power of the tongue, and those who love it will eat its fruit. (Proverbs 18:21 ASV).* I stayed single till 2002 then I met Robert Simmons. Robert was down on his luck and had the most beautiful hazel eyes. He was tall with the military build. We started dating, but Robert had a mystery about himself. I constantly tried to find the mystery. He eventually moved in with me BAD DECISION! We dated. We were on then we were off. Robert was still living that life of; I want to see others. That I want you and not have that commitment type of life. I was not having it. I would tell him to leave but take him back within the same breath.

Whether you are a woman or a man when you keep allowing a person in and out of your life you are giving a person the power to walk on you like a rug. What you need to do is roll your rug up, and say I am no longer your door mat. As my mother use to say, "you have to mean what you say and say what you mean." Can I get a witness? Robert had already transition out the military and was employed at a furniture store. He had moved up the chain so fast that they were wanting to promote him to get his own store. We talked about this, but it was on the table since we were not married.

We continued dating and things was still rocky between us, but we eventually got married. I was in love with this man and he at that time no matter what he said he could sweet talk the icing off a cake. Robert was what I called a Rico Suave.' People loved him and his personality could win them over with his charm. He was very charismatic. Do not get me wrong he was not a bad person he just was smooth as a butter.

Robert took the job in Fayetteville, Nc. and he went on before me as I stayed back for six months. I was employed with the Federal government and was waiting to transfer to North Carolina. They did not transfer me so instead of waiting I got impatient, resign, and relocated to be with him. I was out of a job for about two months, and God blessed me to get on at the Sheriff Department (Want He do It). Favor came my way and things started getting in alignment. We did things together and clubbing was a lot of what Robert wanted to do. We attended service here and there, but we did not commit to any church at that time. We were still without child, and I kept praying since everyone was always asking the big question WHY DON'T YOU HAVE ANY CHILDREN?

People if you see a husband and wife without children do not ask them such questions, because you do not know what might be going on. You are reminding them of not having children. God will open your womb (receive this)!

I felt a tugging in my heart and was tired of hanging out in the clubs with my husband and started searching for my first love which was Jesus Christ as my Lord and Savior. I wanted more and everyday seemed like the tugging got stronger and stronger. I had to find a way to get back in church. I went to different churches, but no church was feeding that desire I was feeling. That is until I got linked up with Christian House of Prayer North Carolina now (Redeeming Love Family Church). I was where I needed to be planted and prayed that my husband turns from his ways and come in. Robert was not hearing it and continue hanging with his friends and coworkers.

Something happens that changed our life and put a strain on our marriage. I was hurt and disappointed all at the same time. I felt my dreams going down the drain. Even though it was not my fault, I took all that shame and guilt that Robert had caused, and I took it personally. I felt like everyone would be looking at me. start pointing fingers and laugh. I had allowed the enemy to speak lies to me. *The thief comes only to steal and kill and destroy. I have come that they may have life and have it in all its fullness (John 10:10 NIV).* This was one of the hardest battles we would have to go through, and we allowed Pastor RT and Louisa McKinney to speak and pray over our lives God was moving.

In the mist of the storms, I learned that I was pregnant and with a baby girl WOW! How many of you know that you intended to harm me, but God intended it all for good? He brought me to this position so I could save the lives of many people (Genesis 50:20 ESV). God will never leave you nor forsake you. If he said it, it shall and will come to pass. God gave us favor and worked it out as we put that behind us. Robert was doing ok but because of the guilt and shame he started staying out and would not come home.

I was now left to go through this pregnancy by myself. I leaned even more on God. I received another tap on my shoulders from God and this time he wanted me. I turned everything over to Him! God has marked me and has called me into the five-fold. *Now these are the gifts Christ gave to the church: the apostles, the prophets, the evangelists, and the pastors and teachers (Ephesians 4:11 NLT).*

I could never forget early prayer at church as the song "Yes" by SHEKINAH GLORY MINISTRY resonated in my spirit and the part where it says, "Sometimes you might have given up some things but are you still willing to say yes?" I screamed and screamed for I know I could no longer run. I wanted him and he wanted me. I was tired of running, and I knew I had to come to him, come to the water to thirst no more. *But whosoever drinketh of the water that I shall give him shall never thirst; but the water that I shall give him shall be in him a well of water springing up into everlasting life (John 4:14 KJV).*

I said yes and never looked back to go back to my old ways of life. My decision to follow Christ was not a decision for Robert. He told me that he did not think I was in it that deep. He did not want that. He was in and out of the house until I had the baby. October 20, 2008, when God brought Patience Bardley Simmons into this world of sin. God knew I needed her, and he gave her to be at the right time.

She was so beautiful, but how was I going to take care of her and give her all the things I did not have as a little girl. Robert was there during deliver as were my mother, and sister Sharon. He only stayed around for a month and eventually that would be the last time he would stay in the home. I still desired him, but God will not violate your will. If this is not something you, are I wanted to do by returning home as the prodigal son did in the bible. I stayed in North Carolina till September 2011. Eventually I asked my sister Loretta, if she could discuss with her husband the possibility of me relocating to Texas with my two-year old daughter to get up on my feet. I resign from a seven-year job and trusted that this was the plans of God.

❧ Chapter VI New Beginning

I had no job and no income coming in, but I was living on the grace of God. Patience and I moved into our one-bedroom home November 2011. I got a job working for the Texas Department Parole office and my journey had begun. One of the things that God does is that he never tells you the end but only wants you to trust him. *Trust in the Lord and lean not to your own understanding in all your ways acknowledge him and he will direct your path (Proverbs 5:5-6 NIV).*

We soon moved into a bigger space in Frisco, Texas and me landing a career in the school district. I was still married to Robert, and it was now since 2015 (12 yrs.) later I finally signed the divorce papers that he had once sent to me in 2013. I could not sign those papers, because I was sold out to Christ and wanted nothing to get in the way from hearing his directions. I had done it my way for so long, but now with a baby I had to be led by Him and Him alone. After prayer and confirmation, I signed the papers and in July 2015, was now divorced.

God spoke to me through John 11 when he called forth Lazarus from the grave. He showed me that even though Lazarus was in the tomb he could still perform a miracle. The people needed to know it was only he that could have bring forth life into any dead situations. How many of you have some dead situations that you need God to bring forth?

God also spoke to me and stated if he were to bring anyone into my life, I could not receive them. I was in covenant with someone else. I was than at peace and continued living my life and raising my daughter. I connected under the leadership of Dr. Edward Conway (One Community Church) Plano, Texas. I got involved with the online ministry. Patience was developing her talents inside church as well as outside. She had basketball skills. I was seeking God concerning my singleness but knew one day in the right season and time God would present me to a man of God. This time I was willing to wait on the Lord since now I could not be selfish due to my daughter was involved.

October 2018, I met a man that I never thought would have come into my life. With the words that I put in the atmosphere to God of, "I am open to whom you have for me," and I accept the love you have for me. Yes, that is what he did Godwin Osatohanmwen showed up lol. We met through a ministry that we were both connected to. We started talking and engaging about the word of God. This was the first time I had been drawn to a man by the spirit and not the flesh. I was not looking at him in a way of I must have him in the bed. I wanted the word that was inside of him that was bearing witness to my spirit. We talked several times on the phone as we were getting to know each other, we finally went on a date as he allowed me into his space as my nerves calmed down.

Godwin is from Nigeria and had come to the USA as the Lord directed him. He was involved in ministry as he is the founder and lead Pastor of Grace and Hope Christian church in Nigeria. Godwin and I would talk about his family as I shared the same about my family. I discovered that he was from a family of seven just as I was from a family of seven. I met his extended family in Houston, his pastors, and friends to know more about him. We continue our friendship as he started asking me questions of Do I smoke? Do I drink? Do I hang out at the clubs, and if I had tattoos? Of course, my answers were not as I thought about the one small tattoo.

I was wondering why he was asking me such questions as I asked. Godwin said to me that he was looking for a wife, and he and I was moving closer. I wanted to be a part of my life as well as me in his life. *He who finds a wife finds a good thing and obtains favor from the LORD (Proverbs 18:22 KJV).*

Godwin had found me and now what does God want me to do with this information? I then started seeking God of this directions as I fast and prayed. My scripture I stood on was *(Proverbs 3:5-6 NIV), Trust in the Lord and lean not to my own understanding in all of ways acknowledge him and he will direct my path.* I went to the throne and spoked with my mother and father about Godwin wanting to marry me. I went to my paster Dr. Conway, Apostle Sean, and Prophetess Beverly Anike for spiritual guidance as well. One of the things in life I had to grow up about is to learn to lean on what directions God was taking me through.

It is not good to rely on the advice of others. I learned through my siblings, who was taking it very hard of me wanting to marry someone, they had no knowledge of. I respected their feelings, but we must know that when God has spoken to you it is good to follow his directions. So, Samuel said: *"Has the LORD as great delight in burnt offerings and sacrifices, as in obeying the voice of the LORD? Behold, to obey is better than sacrifice, and to heed than the fat of rams (1Samuel 15:22 KJV).*

Godwin and I were married March 2019, and as of today we have been married for two-years. I thank God for his grace as this little girl got herself together and pulled up her big girls' panties and stepped out on faith. What do you do with all your brokenness that has been scattered across the world? What do you do when you walk in darkness and are afraid for the light to shine so that you can walk in freedom? What do you do when you have prayed, but it seems like your prayers are not being answered? What do you do when others seem to soar past you, and it should have been you?

What do you do?

Just like an owner of a horse does when his horse has been injured, he takes care of the horse's leg and nurture it back together and reassures the horse he will take good care of him. If the horse's leg is only sprung, the owner has hopes of the horse getting back in the race to finish strong. This is just like our God! If your heart is broken, he can use you even in all your brokenness. He takes those pieces and works it all out for your good. *And we know that in all things God works for the good of those who love him, who have been called according to his purpose (Romans 8:28 NIV).*

In January 2011, God spoke through Dr. McKinney during my ministry ordination and spoke, "out of my misery will become my ministry."

"Sinners Prayer" by Deitrick Haddon

Ye that's without sin, won't you cast the first stone
cus ain't nobody perfect but the man sitting on the throne
but it's about time for us to stop judging one another
stop acting holier than thou and start lifting your brother
but I know all have sinned and come short of its glory
I'm just glad I'm still here to tell the story.

Today, I can honestly say through all the pain and suffering that I have grown through in my life "BROKEN BUT NOT WOUNDED" was birth!
#Gracefully Broken

❧ Conclusion

Since growing through all I have endured in life as a child and young adult. I have learned that the best freedom was freeing all who have wronged me and asking for forgiveness who I have wronged. One of the steps in Celebrate Recovery is a Christ centered 12 step recovery programs for anyone struggling with hurt or pain.

You are only as sick as your secrets and if Satan has you to keep covering up your shame, he will forever have you in darkness. John 8:36 (KJV) If the Son therefore shall make you free, ye shall be free indeed. I was Broken but not wounded.

I want to thank my publisher "Liberation Publishing" out of West Point, Mississippi, for having so much patience in making this book come to life. I thank you for pushing me and encouraging me to allow my testament to be a testimony for others, who may not know how to break free of their guilt, sin, and darkness, back into the marvelous light 1 Peter 2:9 (Bible Gateway) God bless you 100-fold in Jesus Christ's name!

Minister Charlene Bardley Osatohanmwen
Contact me at
charlene41simmons@gmail.com

❦ Appendix

My Childhood Home

Broken But Not Wounded

My Family

S. D. Lee High School – Columbus Mississippi